INSPIRATIONS©

MESSAGES FROM AN EARTH HEALER
NEW THOUGHT FOR TIMES OF GREAT CHANGE

WRITTEN BY
CHERYL GALL

INSPIRATIONS

Published by LightWay Services
Prescott, Arizona 86303

Library of Congress Control Number: 2020915585

ISBN: 978-0-578-74199-4

First Printing 2020

HERE IS TO THE NEW EARTH AND ALL OF HUMANITY THAT AWAKENS!

Acknowledgements

Mom, you inspired me through the toughest times to persevere. I am the woman today because of you.

Erin, you have been my rock, my mirror and biggest supporter. Even when I struggled with the belief I could not accomplish such a feat on my own. But you always stood by me and believed in my dreams.

To my best friend Shirley Wolf. You are amazing! Thank you for being an anchor, sharing your light and being who you are. I love you with all my heart!! I will always be grateful for you being such a huge part of my life.

CONTENTS

Contents

continued...

CONTENTS

CONTENTS

INTRODUCTION

Welcome to my book of Inspirations, self-empowerment and motivational daily words during our ascension. Despite an upheaval on the planet, humanity will always continue to search for motivation, love and connection within ourselves, others, and most importantly, with source.

Our natural state of being has never changed. But from lifetimes of programming and conditioning, there is a profound awakening, which requires one to discern what is in their heart, to trust it, and to let go or re-program the part that is not organic and natural.

The shackles of our old thoughts and belief systems are now falling off. Without looking back and being mindful to not to put the shackles back on, we step into the New Earth. An On High life that truly connects all life to Father and Mother God. Creators we were born to be, conscious creators we are now set ourselves free.

This book was written with the intention to promote good health and wellness. By simply reading these pages, the words of upliftment, encouragement and mindfulness will no doubt raise your vibration. When something is done just a little bit differently each day, the reality of your choice also begins to change.

Moving from a denser place of thinking such as fear, worry, lack, self-doubt, will allow the reader to think in a lighter place, thus reducing our own self-imposed limitations. We gently move out of our comfort zone of accepting everything just as. Even the quality of our own life will greatly improve on every level. When this happens, the energetic value that increases within you also permeates through you and outward and affects all life, especially Mother Earth.

Everyone on this planet was taught to obey a system of controls that rules within them. An inorganic programming that contains and confines the human's experience in a 3- dimensional world.

All the dreams we have had of super powers, super heroes, helping each other on such a grander scale were removed from our thoughts and only appeared to be a fantasy or some distant dream.

Changing our patterns of programming, i.e. beliefs, thoughts and rituals, will remove us from confinement and allow ourselves to experience that supernatural realm that truly exist with each and everyone of us.

I hope you find as much enjoyment reading each page as I did writing it.

I have such profound love for you on your journey of awakening to the awe of what life is truly is.

It is magnificent, it is radiant, it is pure LOVE!

Quiet

For today, try to take a few minutes and just stop the chatter, the noise in your mind. Be still and just let go of it all. This heavy, dense energy keeps us weighed down. For a moment, breathe the light into your body and allow yourself to just be still, quiet. This is a perfect way to connect all of you. The part that you cannot see that is your soul self. Feel the love from Pachamama and all the elements here that want to share and be reunited with you. Just for a moment...

Surrender

Be ready to take the next step to go to the next level. Know that you have to surrender every bit of ego. Be prepared to release old stories, old luggage, old energies, things that no longer serve you. Surrender ALL and become the I AM.

Kindness

Be kind to yourself. Let it go. Let the love pour out of your heart and just let it go.

Mirroring You

Practice Meditation. Practice Mindfulness, regardless of the challenge. See your own behaviors and commence change where it feels not in alignment with your higher self. Take responsibility by just being who you are. Pure love. Light that is connected to Source. Practice allowing to feel your own natural state as a high vibrational being. Eat clean for your vessel needs high frequency foods not feeding the mind with addictions. Bless your food and change its frequency with love and gratitude.

Embrace Change

These are really simple changes in our everyday life style that we need to be accountable for. It impacts all of us collectively. Do we continue to contribute to the matrix and be the slave or do we open our hearts and practice with perspective? Identify the fear inside us that controls us. It has been ingrained in humanity for a long time. This is an invisible chain that keeps us tethered and at a low vibration.

The Observer

Just observe what's around you.
No need for action, or siding.
It still creates division within yourself and humanity.
What is it that you really want?
Freedom? Heath? Wealth?
No need to take a side.

Creating Space for You

Clearing yourself all the limitations of programming will
open space for more creator light.
Focus on just what you desire.
Spend your energy wisely and sensibly

Protection

Do not allow anything to affect your high vibration unless it is an experience you choose to have.

Be Positive

Did you know a negative thought cancels out your
positive thoughts?
You have 16 seconds to cancel out the negative thought.
We truly have the ability to decide our path.
Choose to make it an amazing day!!
Love is always here for you!

Healing

How beautiful to challenge the change! It is an opportunity to see very clearly the wrongness we all have done. Now we reverse the numbness to become all feeling and respond to it. It is simply by acts of kindness that imprints on every person who receives it.

It is bounded by no expectations or contracts. Giving, compassion, caring is just being simply a human stripped of all darkness and heavy energy. It is to be of light and love.

It takes deep cleansing, deep, conscious work to identify each program. Then remove it and replace it. It takes will and courage. It is taking ownership of who you are and initiative to make the changes that feel right for you.

This is more powerful on a collective level.

It takes work to accomplish this. Now is the time to create the change within which results in a change in our reality.

Love prevails.

You the Creator

Do you know your thoughts are faster than the speed of light? Did you know that your thoughts create the world you live in? Do you know, as a human, how powerful you are?

Collectively we can and are changing the way we live and how we treat this planet.

It is truly amazing and beautiful!

Waking Up

Ever wonder who we really are in this world?

This planet, so special and beautiful. How do we get so involved in the little things of life that distracts us from such beauty?

Missing the connection to who we really are.

Take a moment and breathe...feel it, see it, smell it.

Know in your heart that the little things during your day perhaps are not so important.

Look at what really matters and feel the gratitude that we have. Such an amazing opportunity to experience and make changes.

Stillness

For today, try to take a few minutes and just stop the chatter, the noise in your mind. Be still and just let go of it all. This heavy, dense energy keeps us weighed down. For a moment breathe the light into your body and allow yourself to just be still, quiet. This is a perfect way to connect all of you. The part that you cannot see that is your soul self. Feel the love from Pachamama and all the elements here that want to share and be reunited with you. Just for a moment...

Responsibility

The Changes on Earth are up to you!
Love, Wisdom and Service!

Great Change is Now

In the coming days of the end to a new beginning, the world is enveloped with a love that all life never felt before. Every man, woman and child has shifted their perspective to a higher dimensional life. With full awareness and choice.

Total alignment will be found in each and every one of us. Smiling becomes a norm and is desired all the time, no matter where we are. Our hearts are open and pure with the ability to feel all heart beats as they are one, pulsing with the creator.

Our current experience will soon be viewed simply as the process of evolution of humanity. What we desire is manifesting the freedom of all life and to be completely released of this old paradigm.

Around this world and in the multi-verse that we Humans are awake and full of love. We are ready to step completely and divinely in the new realm of higher dimensional living. We embrace and demonstrate compassion, forgiveness and love effortlessly.

Simplicity dominates and represents being present and aware of every breathe, every thought and action we take.

Today and every day is a beautiful celebration of the Christ energy, a birth that brought us the gift of love and unity for all life.

And so it is.

Polarized –
Which One are You?

Duality expands more each and every moment.
It's not about taking sides.
It's following your own enlightened path.

Life

The conscious breath of every
moment is living in the present.

Success!

Dreams were taught to fantasize and live with limitations. Imagination was a way to incorporate a belief system of impossible reality. Know that all creations thought by you are never limited. They are infinite realms of all possibilities.

$\mathcal{LOVE}$

The force of love is within all souls that commands the
creation with the heart.

Shedding Old Stories

Temptation is not of love but the ego desperately trying to hang on. Old patterns of habits programmed so deeply in our lifetimes will eventually fall way. It is up to your consciousness, your will, to want change and let go of control. We are home with Source now.

Healing from Loneliness

Holidays and cultural beliefs systems can bring on a loneliness to be with family. Old wounds will open once again and offer many opportunities to change the reality that continues to play over and over again. This time, this year, I changed vibration to create a different reality. Though part of me, the ego, wanted to reply the pain and loneliness that I entertain, it was at this point, this year, that I needed to go much deeper to understand that I am the only one subjecting myself to this pain by feeding the same old story. I had not honored this part of me. Which denied me to experience myself to the fullest as an ascended master.

Today, I honor myself. I acknowledge that I am surrounded by love, comfort, and all life that resonates with my heart. I also call on my guardian angels and guides to assist me in any way they can to accompany me on my journey.

Want to Feel Good?

Why do we subject ourselves around others who do not feel good to be around? There is no honor to the self if others cannot see you and your light. We sometimes have to take a deep breath and break patterns of traditions and beliefs systems in order to re-create a path that allows infinite light and love. Then our ascension will take flight.

Need Change Now

Keeping ourselves anchored to beliefs and or traditions that are not a vibrational match will only prevent oneself from taking flight to the next level of our evolution. You cannot fly if you have weights that keep you down. Free will. Honor thyself, love thyself and set yourself free.

Letting Go of Attachments

Holding on to people and things
Causes humans the most pain and suffering.
Detachment is the self-mastery of infinite love of all.

Setting Your Attentions Daily

You can alter your day by altering your thinking. Set your intentions first thing in the morning once you rise, before being totally back in your body. Before your resistance gets in the way:

1. Get the momentum going by declaring your current state of gratitude of all you have now.

2. Choose to be happy.

3. Once there is silence, feel the amazing power of your innate self rise up and come through you.

This is the most important part of you. YOUR LIGHT!

4. Allow your higher self to speak through you, feel through you and act from you.

This is your connection to Source. Your I AM self.

Intend to create with breath, with your higher self at the helm of your ship. Your resistance will be gone! Manifesting successfully means you are connected to Source.

Our manifestations will come easier and easier once you identify the old programming that is interferring, then clearing it, thus making a place to be filled with love and light.

It is up to you to let it go, let go of control, and let the sails be pushed by the winds of your desire. Let the ego step aside to get out of your way.

5. It will not and should not matter how it comes, but TRUST, it will. Feel the excitement of what is about to happen in your life with such ease and grace.

Another way to think about letting go of control to manifest easier. Ask yourself how are things working for you now? If you are not content and or tired of trying, and you really really desire change, then it is up to you to try a different vibration YOU are creating.

Feeling Lifted

RISE, RISE, RISE. Be above all the division of choices presented to you in this dense paradigm. There are no walls, no divisions, no compartmentalization. Everything has always been designed to divide humanity by choosing a side to something: Division is the allowance of investing your powerful energy and claiming someone else's beliefs, that are not your beliefs. We allowed ourselves to be hijacked.

Step into your power my dear sisters and brothers.

Rise above this noise and see the bigger picture of what is happening. Make time. Get out of the tunnel vision. This is a planetary event that is happening now. Ask yourself if you are in a division, does it feel good? Do you think it will change the world by joining a side?

Rise above it all. Raise your consciousness, your vibration. Just focus on love, kindness, forgiveness. Set the example of who you are. Allow yourself to feel the light of freedom and love that is pouring onto Mother Earth. This higher frequency of love we call it evolving. It is here now. Do the work. Set the example of removing the division by loving messages. Be LOVE.

Be Powerful!

Keep shining your light!! You are a powerful luminous being. Your light removes darkness. Shine, shine, shine!!

Attuning to Higher Frequencies

Raising your vibration is the ability to hear beyond the lower dimensional realm. It is hearing the voice of creator within.

Evolved!

Expand your consciousness and be unconditional love. It is time to allow yourself to let go of outside systems that offer beliefs that are not of high frequency. These beliefs continue to lead to polarization within. They do not assist in your ascension. Take charge and tap into your own soul self wisdom to unite with your I AM.

You are magical, powerful and of pure LOVE.

Challenge

Lower thoughts keep you in a place to survive
vs higher thoughts allow you to THRIVE!
Your choice.

Crossroads

At this point of time, if your thoughts of fear, worry, doubt or confusion take hold of you, then you need to take hold of this programming and focus on your own powerful light. You can make a difference here on Earth.

Today, be the change. Set the example of being evolved, by being compassionate and loving.

You have to do the work.

Creating

Everything you do with your breathe, your food, your drink, your actions, your thoughts affects your vibration.

Lifted

Step into the wonderment of the sounds beyond your wildest dreams and hear the angels sing. Feel the vibrations of the ocean waves and the cleaning of the solar winds as you morph into love and light!

Going Home

We are here to evolve into oneness.
Going home is acknowledging Source within.

Being Present

Just for today, I will rise like the sun, breathe like the wind and float like the clouds.

Becoming Authentic

As humanity rewires self for the exploration of the new self, peace will prevail, and love will conquer all.

Be true to yourself and all others will see you.

Healing Light Upon You!

Light brings us transparency to see the shadows that have been hidden for lifetimes. A time of releasing, healing and raising your vibration to quantum levels of light!

Connecting to Yourself

The only separation you feel, see and think of another being, is merely revealing the separation of your higher self within you.

You are tremendously loved. Let go of the fear, the anger that feeds the very source that has kept you in density for lifetimes.

Feel this amazing light coming into us all.
It's simply infinite love, freedom and joy transforming humanity.

It keeps getting better everyday.

You Are Powerful!

Remember who you are and how powerful you can be.

Every thought, word or action has energy attached to it. It affects not only yourself, but the other person, expanding outward the world.

You are that powerful!

Be The Light

Our higher self is so much stronger than our ego self. It persevered no matter how much we separated from ourselves. The awakening is happening. The light is transmuting the old energies. This had once dominated the programming for lifetimes.

Now, no more.

Today, I will practice just being light.

Unified

Now we rise, rise, rise together. Stronger in numbers.
Stronger of the light and love. We now take over the
guardianship of Gaia. Our beautiful Mother Earth.

And so it is.

And so it is.

And so it is.

Amen.

Stepping Out!

Time has served only one purpose. Measuring productivity. It only functioned in the lower density of form, of material. Moving away from old energies removes the function of time. It does not serve the higher realms of your work.

Discernment

Learn to identify old beliefs systems that are from present day and past life unresolved issues. These issues can make us feel stuck, depressed, and not able to pursue our dreams to live to our hearts content. Learn to identify where the programming is within you and how to take control of your life.

Feel Life

Stand next to a tree and feel the heartbeat. Feel the joy of the ground beneath your feet. Feel yourself melting into the earth. Mother Earth, Gaia, Releasing and breathing, releasing and breathing. Become one with all life around you. The trees, the earth, the wind.

You!

Learning to be a master in life is not about perfection. You are already perfect. It is about embracing the non-physical reality of who you are. When you do this, you will understand that the physical is not as difficult. It is temporary and a beautiful gift. Mastering this means to live with non-attachment to the physical, practice forgiveness and unconditional love to all life just as much as you love yourself. It is about taking ownership of the life we have created and moving forward with good intentions. We are luminous beings of light and love. This is our natural state.

Light Permeates

As we expand with light, our own shadows are revealed. Like reliving the past of a blacked- out memory. It is temporary and now clearing. Ascension awaits you

Unified to Oneness

You make a difference not only in your life but everything around you. Taking your power and manifesting with the highest intentions for not only self but all that are affected will undoubtedly come true. Be patient. Spirit lives and thrives in all of us. The only way we create is co-create with Spirit. We are not and have never been alone here.

Embrace each other.

Love each other.

Being in physical form is a choice and a gift.

Love Thyself

Breathe deeply, smile brightly, love infinitely.

House Cleaning

Know that in order to ascend on our path of enlightenment, one needs to do the due diligence in cleaning and clearing the vessel. Clearing and cleaning means to de-program, transmute and release these energies that are not of the higher conciousness thought. If we do not focus on healing of these energies, it will continue to affect and influence the new thoughts in the lower frequency.

Compassion

Loving is with detachment. Their story is not your story. Respect all souls' journeys.

Honor others, regardless of their choices.

Good Health

Clearing and cleaning your vessel applies to the manifestations of that heavy energy in your physical body. Eating clean food, staying hydrated and being mindful of your thoughts, all play a part in your own evolution. Are you allowing self to be directed by your heart or mind?

Breathe

Stay awake and aware and be present in the moment to enjoy this life.

Accept the fact that living in duality does not work, and go within to connect to all that is, you will see what I am talking about.

.

Shifting Perspective

We can get caught up in the day to day dramas; the looping of a story that binds us to the bottom of the world of dense energy. Releasing every day and clearing allows you to adjust to new thinking, with your heart. Your cosmic self and infused with love. This in turn washes away the fear base thinking. Light always removes darkness.

LOVE!

Feel gratitude, joy and happiness. It is a choice!

New Thought, New Dimension

Timelines are falling away. The reality of what was yesterday, is different today and will continue to change every day for now on. Be mindful of not reacting rather, go into breath and ground to what is your current state of reality that you create for today. Look for old timelines that could pull you back in the lower energies; that you have worked for life times to try to get out of.

All That There Is

The higher energies will show you your own transformation into your true state of being. Everything is connected. Cause and effect. Mindfulness and acknowledge what surfaces is to be released. This will accelerate your total merge with your I AM presence.

Compassion

Giving any of your energy in an unloving way to a person, place or thing will continue to keep you separated from your own heart and higher self.

Compassion, Love and Forgiveness to Yourself.

Focusing on another's faults keeps you distracted from going within and doing your own work.

It's time to be at peace. First with ourselves. Then each other.

Always Loving You!

Feeling Fragmented

Channel high frequencies while transmuting low. Shifting thoughts from fear to thoughts of love. Be in stillness rather fragmentation. The quality of life should be rich with divine love rather than bits and pieces.

Owning Your Light

You do not have to take a side to anything.
If at anytime you are confused and do not know who or what to believe, then take that time you use looking on the outside for answers and go within.

It is all inside of you.

Breathe, think and you will create.

Love and you will live life the fullest.

Freedom to fly.

It is not up to anyone else to tell you how to live your life

Dig deep and find that illumined truth inside and become light.

Be the example of an enlighten being.

LOVE

Love is boundless, infinite and complete.

Healing

Love is healing.

Merging to Oneness

Dear Creator, I allow myself the total merging of all of my selves to your divine light. A unifying alignment that brings me home to your arms of light and love.

Compass

As you experience a multi-dimensional life, you will always illuminate your current state of frequency.

Ripple Effect

You are the source of the ripple that was created from the vibration of what you are thinking.

Be love!

Collective Consciousness Heals

We share so many wonderful things. We remind each other of our thoughts, words and action. But mindful that low thoughts affect not only ourselves but this very energy radiates out to our surroundings. To our loved ones, neighbors and the planet. All as one. All are one.

Reflection

Practicing stillness is self-love. Take the time to be complete. Experience wholeness by feeling the vibration with all of you rather than with fragmentation.

Be wholeness, be holiness, be love.

Oneness I AM

Just for today, practice wholeness. Connect with your I AM presence and feel the immense love that connects all of us together. The power within us collectively changes the reality we are in to one that is expansive of pure light and love from the On High. Be still, be still, be still and feel the love.

Reflection

Be mindful of your vibrations. These are projected out and affects all. Transmute low vibrational thoughts to forgiveness, love and joy. We feed the same story when we promote it, even if it may be one not in the highest and best.

Magnify!

Light illuminates the darkness and together as one we can change this.

Regroup, Reflect and Reinforce!

No matter how you do it, staying connected to higher self first thing in the morning really changes your day. Set it with your intent on how you want your day.

It works every time!!

Riding the Wave~

Trust and have faith that the journey you are on, that you have created, is precious and filled with experiences, knowledge and wisdom. This allows one to see more clearly, to love more freely and to forgive yourself and others.

Just an Illusion

Know in your heart that all is well, and that fear is just a man-made illusion to control and manipulate. This is the root of creating the heavy energy. You get to choose!!

Changing the Dial

Today, joy, calmness and peace are within. Some days it will appear as the same "stuff" that you cannot control. But how you handle it differently will reflect from your own growth. What a wonderful thing to see!

Forgiveness

When we share our thoughts, fears, worries and anger, we also share that vibration to others. If sharing a low vibrational thought, transmuting the energy attached to it first will not be toxic.

Intentions Set!

Collectively and individually we are all accountable for how we think and create energies. Together this how we bring our planet back to full consciousness.

For today, take 5 minutes to take three deep breaths down to your belly and exhale with the intent of releasing all the heaviness, stress, and noise within. Decide how you want to feel today, regardless of what is going on. Mother Earth is taking her deep breathes. Connect with her and feel the infinite high energy, love and joy. Feel the Father Sun and his rays fall upon you and illuminate your total beautiful self.

Ascending

In order to work with the 5th dimensional energies, you have to leave the 3rd dimensional self. How do you do that? Meditate, pray, whatever it takes to allow yourself to shift and become adjusted to the higher frequencies. Our bodies are dense, so it takes patience and great self-care and understanding that the headaches and pains, flu like symptoms you may be having is the adjustment period. Just rest and allow it all to balance out then work a little more. Gaia is holding the space and grounding us while we shift into the new paradigm.

Change

To explore more, simply practice shifting your consciousness to the higher realm.

Inside Out

All resistance felt is just a lesson for us. A mirror. Look around at your resistance. This is associated with feelings of fear, anger, guilt, sadness. It is a disconnect with your higher self and of low frequency thoughts. What do you see? What is it you need to learn to put it all back together again?

Just breathe and let go of it. Watch life flow as it should be and that things always turn out better than we tried to plan in the 3D. You are not alone and are connected to all that is. Gratitude, Joy and Love is with you!

Take Flight!

Expand your wings of light and soar across the cosmos with your heart leading you.

It is infinite, joyous and free!!!

Easier Path

A time to celebrate the releasing of your own shadows and seek the path of least resistance.

Embracing Light

Walking your path is not to know where you are or where you are going, but trust that it is your path to freedom and fearlessness.

Warriors of Light!

Carry your sword of light to touch all of those who look for help to be ignited by the flame of love.

Step forward courageously and trust that what you are doing now is better than how you were doing it before. Because it is a different vibration you are creating!

Vibrations

Changing your rhythm changes your creations.
What tune are playing now?

Breaking Free From Madness

The human soul craves for freedom as the lower body had been anchored in heaviness.

Free of Chains

Allow the stars to light your path, your breath transmutes density and may your wings expand to fly distances you have only imagined.

Leadership

Be in control rather than be controlled by limiting beliefs and old programs that no longer serve you.

Letting GO

Close your eyes for a just a moment and tune into Spirit. Feel the energy of the life all around you. This is a Cosmic Connection. The I AM.

Pillar of Light

Despite all the upheaval going on Mother Earth, hold your light.

Be aware but not engage.

Every time there is an engagement with the old energies, we feed into it. It weakens your own vibration.

Know how important and powerful you are. Be with community of like-minded. Stay focus on the real truth. Love mirrored outward.

Light that protects and is impenetrable. Dissolving old energies.

Imagine your light being this light house that anchors in Mother Earth and radiates outward, around the Earth and in the multi-verse.

So many distractions are designed to hurt, take life and keep us separated.

Hold your truth, hold your heart and love infinitely.

Transparency

Feel the veils get thinner and thinner as we all embrace the experience of the dimensions collapsing. Our consciousness expands, and we truly become united as one.

Time for Change

Have you ever thought some of the habits in your life may not be good for you? Why do you allow them to control you? Are you a slave to your own mind? Coffee? Alcohol? Sugar? Drama and stories?

I challenge you to take one habit, that is not so healthy for you and replace it with a moment of stillness. Just enjoy being you without trying to fill it with something else.

Take a walk, enjoy being in nature, play with your animals (or someone else's, LOL), smile and wave at neighbors. Create a new habit of just enjoying you!!

Create with intention in all things you do.

Freedom

Be mindful of what we have allowed ourselves to be subjected to.

Choose to be free, choose to be love. Eat healthy, and if you cannot eat high vibrational foods, then simply transmute the density and charge it with light higher than what exists. Choose what thoughts and energy wave your creating, that ripples inward then out. Allow your higher self to integrate with your corporeal body. Your cells will respond to your light. Say your I AM and full name 3 times to command the integration now.

Making Change

15-minute meditations during your day will assist you to adjust to the higher frequencies coming in daily. Be gentle with yourself. Know that all is well.

Galactic Human Emerging

Be in a state of being by feeling the joy of it
Rather than in a state of wanting.

Get Focus

Any thought, word or action of a low vibration will interfere with your ability to use your intuition clearly.

Pulling up the Anchors

Let go with what you know
There is enough for everyone!

Honor Thy Self

Create time for self-nurturing, being out in nature.
Breathe. Become aware and be present. Stay in gratitude.

Releasing

Time to let go of all resistance no matter what it is.
It's a reminder to just keep working at it, layer by layer.

Be The Light

Be independent and trust your intuition to know your truth. You are your own authority, a powerful creator of form, unless you choose to surrender it to others.

Build community to make changes collectively, that benefit humanity and honor Mother Earth.

Question everything.

No one, place or event will set you free

This has to be your will and your higher self integrated within you all the time to release the chains of heaviness.

Change Your Frequency, Change Your Reality

What are you doing differently now to change that frequency of habit...same patterns that make the same reality you are creating? Want FREEDOM?

Pray, meditate for peace, freedom, abundance. It's right there. Just focus on what you really really want. Be patient. Practice being, doing that you normally don't. Set yourself free. You are not alone.

Emergence

The emergence of self sheds old beliefs from self-serving to being of service.

The healing aspect of our evolution is that we can allow our hearts to soar even higher than ever before. No judgement, no pain and most of all no fear. Be who you are meant to be and honor thyself as if you would to your God Self. Now integrated with Oneness.

A creator that manifest from the pureness of your heart, for the goodness of all.

Getting Into Alignment

To access higher dimensions, your emotional, physical, mental energetic bodies have to be cleared and be at the same vibration. Control the chatter and dive into the realms of chaos to clear and be free of enslaved thought forms that serve you no longer.

Home

New Earth is also a new way of living. No guidebook, rules or fear. Feel with all of your body to make a decision. Tap in to your innate self, Akashic records, all multi-dimensional lives and past life of knowledge, wisdom and truth. It is already there within you. It is calm, joyful and free. No limits. Feel love in all that you do.

Energies New Earth

What you did and what you know from yesterday will not work today. Step out of your comfort zone and feel the infinite wind on your face, the father sun on your shoulders and the softness of Mother Earth anchoring you to stand tall.

When you change your patterns, you will create new ones. Create consciously and with love!

Flying Free!

Swan dive into the ocean of love and set yourself free!

Powerful You Are!

As the old paradigms continue to disappear and new frequencies are set forth, reality changes ever so quickly by the power of your thoughts and emotions.

Be mindful of your creations.

Blossoming To Fullest Potential

Time feels to stand still, it feels not real. Floating, quietly, drifting in and out. The surface is crumbling and clearing the way for the newness of life to be planted and grow. Your inner quietness is the seed that is about to germinate to create the life on Mother Earth that you have always wanted.

Freedom, love, joy and peace!

Being Present

Stop what you are doing and breathe. Breathe in life force energy and see the roots of Gaia come through the ground and wrap her arms around you. Grounding you, calming you and always loving you.

Gratitude

Bath in the moonlight of Mother Moon,
Mama Killa, Express gratitude.

Being Lifted

Feel the beating of your heart. Feel the breath move all the way down to your belly. Feel life in all its newness. Feel the joyfulness in all that you do and who you are.

Awareness

Change one single thought (vibration) and change your reality. Each and everyone one of us is a powerful creator. Create mindfully!

Being in Awe of it All!

Bounds of beauty in all of its glory is right in front of us.
See Mother Earth as a powerful conscious living being!

Feeling Deeply

Gratitude comes from the depths of our soul. It is not just a thank you card, your hand to your heart, or even a bow of your head. It is so much more than that.

Be Infinite Creators

Separation of self is supported in multiple ways. All designed to keep you from being in a state of gratitude.

LOVE!

Gratitude is not a state of expectancy. It is honor, love and sincerity all wrapped in a rainbow of light!

Be Powerful

Words defy all human's behavior.
Think first before you create.

The Journey

Step in the waves of light that penetrate your total existence on every energetic level. Swim with each stroke with determination that your destination is not the goal, rather it is how you swim.

Connected

Every breathe that you feel that goes all the way down is the very moment your higher self, your I AM self is within you.

Healing Childhood

Have you noticed that humans are drawn to the sun and its rays? Not just for the warmth and light, but the spiritual enlightenment of stillness, silence, love and freedom. The sun comforts us as if the rays wraps us like a blanket and then we know all is well.

Being Home

Practicing silence is the biggest gift to the creator. Because then and only then, we are not distracted by a person, place or thing. It creates a complete connection to our higher self.

Listen within.

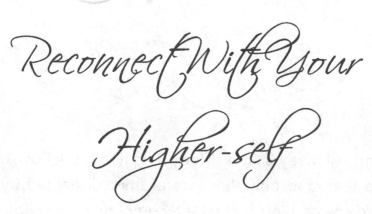

Reconnect With Your Higher-self

Making time to go outside to be with Mother Earth shows the distance we have drawn from Creator and ourselves.

Gratitude Of
Who You Are

I celebrate all of you in your most amazing light. Your energy signature is the most unique in this multi-verse. I feel your vibrations and joy in your heart.

Now it is time for you to see yourself.

Daily Habits of Mindfulness

Free of news watching.

Free of programs that don't feel good.

Free of shows that feel it pulls on your attention/energy and distracts me.

Unplug the modem at night.

Use speaker or headphones more often on cell phones.

Turn off phone at night.

Drink filtered water.

Make your own toothpaste.

Eat organic, despite costs, make adjustments (The thought of every product I pick up has been sprayed over and over with insect killer/repeller. (Think of the bigger picture of your health, not just immediate).

... Daily Habits of Mindfulness

Reduce the sugar to minimal amounts to none in your daily consumption. (Watch yourself when you crave as it is an addiction, especially to our children).

Attach the vibration of love to everyone and everything you do. It will make a difference even if you cannot see it. Everyone does feel it.

Protect our planet by picking up trash, even if it is not yours.

Stop and help a stranger in need.

Be in a place of service rather self-serving.

Question everything. Time to re-create.

Look for real leaders to help humanity rather than those with a political agenda of power.

Mediate, meditate, meditate. A state of practice to be in higher consciousness at all times.

Love, Love, Love.

Reprogram yourself to do things out of the box, to feel free, joyful and happy.

You are not a slave anymore, unless it is your choice.

Taking Flight

The breath of mortality ceases as the wings appear on your back. Take flight and truly feel life as it should be.

God Self Speaks

When I become stillness, I feel, I hear and I see with such great beauty and joy that life is truly breath taking. I AM all that there is. Unified in love. Complete and in gratitude.

Tunnel Vision

Look at the bigger picture of everything to keep your perspective. It is all connected.

Have Faith

Instead of trying to find the reason or an explanation of a situation, just release the fact that you are working with the universe in obtaining the explanation and will be received at the right time.

Becoming Powerful

It's all about timelines and what or which one you choose to be on.

It makes all the difference in your reality and yours alone. What do you choose? Light or Darkness? Love or fear?

You are allowed to step out of the paradigm that keeps you trapped.

All the dreams you have had to be free, can and will come true if you change your programming.

Stop turning your power over to self appointed authorities that have a darker agenda.

You are incredibly powerful, beautiful and free if you and the collective make the choice.

I love you more than you know

Trust

As you begin to morph and change your humanness, there is a sense of excitement and joy that you know all is well and exciting. Feel the calmness of letting go of all the heaviness we have carried for life times and feel complete, free and joyful!

Mindfulness Creators

Stay in a place that feels good.
This is conscious creating and experiencing by choice.
By staying focused on what you chose will attract the very
same energy continuously.

Stay Focused
On What Matters

Any thought, word or action of a low vibration will interfere with your ability to use your intuition clearly.

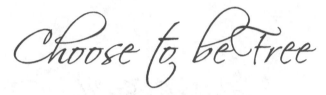
Choose to be Free

Reprogram yourself to do things out of the box, to feel
free, joyful and happy.
You are not a slave anymore, unless it is your choice.
Always from my heart to yours, I love you!

Compassion

Human kindness is priceless.
It is infinite love and unconditional.

Connected

Love is everywhere! Can you feel the hearts softening? What use to be fear, is now compassion. What an incredible journey to experience this shift fully awake!

Priceless To Feel

There is no greater joy than to be present
and feel everything.
Experience everything, love everything.

Free Will

Only you can make the choice to determine
how you want to feel.

Connected to Source

Freedom compels you to take a swan dive and let go of all limiting thoughts. Set yourself free to fly!

Becoming You

My heart speaks the truth. My feelings never lie.
My mind can be deceptive.
Which system do you live your life by?
Can you integrate all to become a balanced
divine galactic human?

Be The Shaman

Take just a moment and breathe.
Much chaos around you and it feels surreal.
Like watching it from outside looking in.
Be aware but not a part of.
Keep your vibration high and full of love regardless.

Clarity

Detach yourself from the imbalances that have led you astray. Keep clear of your own path rather than walking another's.

Unified

To be free is to not volunteer enslavement. It is a choice.
Together we can make an impact.
Unity, consciousness and love.

Prayer For Today

Dear Source, creator of all that there is. I ask your assistance of clearing my vessel of all limiting beliefs, programming, traumas that do not serve me any longer. This means that whatever I engage in that creates resistance in myself is something I need to face, honor it and let it go. I allow myself to be in alignment today with more light than ever.

My own personal upheavals are never about a person, place or thing outside of me. It is how I am reacting to this situation and the real causation is going on within me. Past life and present life issues.

I AM releasing.

I will acknowledge what is coming up, even if I cannot identify it, just know it is mine and I own it. I will take great care of myself. Resting, meditating, whatever that is to bring stillness in to honor the great light that I AM. It is all about healing. Just like Mother Earth. She is also going through major changes and releasing.

In order to create the new paradigm together, I must be responsible, and not bring the old programming with me. I need to strive to be clear, loving to myself and others at all times.

I wish many blessings to self on this beautiful day. I will breathe deeply, love infinitely and know it is getting better collectively as we have each other!

Change Is Imminent

Changing your thoughts will change your reality

Just taking one pattern of thoughts, a belief that you repeat the pattern daily and changing it to something that is un-limited will alter the frequency emitted from you. This creates a different reality. A reality of choice.

One Thought At A Time

If there is something in your life that is not working, and you seek change, why not try something different and become creators with intention? Change your beliefs, thoughts, feelings and it will change your creations.

Patience

We cannot merge in totality of the collective until we can merge all of ourselves. Pulling the fragments and distortions of frequencies from our thoughts, words and actions and then maintaining this vibration to embrace the I AM presence.

Keep practicing a place of stillness, no matter how noisy it may be. Be patient. It is work. We all have to do it to make the change for a new reality. One of infinite light, love, Divine Grace in all that we do.

Take Charge Of Your Life

Every day is a new day, it is up to you to decide if you choose to carry old thoughts and heavy energies into your creation.

Becoming Transparent

In any part of one's life, all things become visible when there is a lack of harmony, balance and love.

Being mindful is creating thoughts with higher vibrations versus your ego interfering with your creations.

Be it work or play, it affects us all.

Quietness

The simpler life is made,
the easier to hear your inner guidance.

Programs

A belief is a library of control mechanisms that create your reality to be distorted or clear. What do you believe in today?

You are Light

You are the only one on this planet that carries a unique energy signature. Not like anyone else. Merge your frequency to the Central Sun and feel yourself ignite with pureness.

New Day...

New times, new programming. How do you want to start your day now? Create wisely, with love and always with good intentions

Breath

Hear the mountain calling your name to climb it. Allow yourself to become the mountain and attune your silence to hers. Allow yourself to melt into her power of sacredness and love. Respect the shared vision of what you can now see with such great clarity.

Being in Rhythm with Mother Earth

Dancing in the rain is always a celebration to be joyful, free and happy. Make a date to dance at the next rain.

Celebrate

Now is not about spending your powerful energy on the chaos. It still keeps you there. Direct your light to creating the life you truly desire. Allow yourself to have complete freedom of your soul and take flight.

Being in Love

Love creates amazing experiences. Short and long term. It is not about holding on to what is transforming but to live that experience with gratitude, knowing that detachment allows all to fully experience without contract, limitations and or fear.

Acknowledge Self

There is only one of you in the multiverse. Everyone knows about you except you. Stand in your light and love yourself like no other. Feel the truth of you and allow it to surface with great clarity.

Ascension Symptoms

It may seem everything is coming apart (mind). But it is actually feeling like it's coming together (heart). There is calmness, like floating on an ocean.

Your letting go, your allowing with little to no resistance. Like the Condor ready to take flight.

You hear the white noise or high pitches. Sometimes it sounds like angelic music.

You FEEL everything. Deeply touched by simple acts of kindness by others and desiring to do the same.

Your becoming more expansive with light. You are transforming. You are becoming your raw self that reveals your true foundation of your existence. LOVE.

Wings Of Light

The most incredibly powerful force in
existence of the multiverse.
Being a creator. You are this magnificent
being of light, love.
Welcome home.

New Awakening

The profoundness of it all can be overwhelming
Regardless of the spiritual maturity.

It only eases in with less confusion
Every day we break further and further way from the
prisons of our own creations
To touch the depth-ness of what love truly is.

Peace Be Within You

Be in stillness
Breathe deeply
Gratitude

A Solar Wave

Keep hanging on. Timelines are merging. Dealing with a great deal of forgetfulness. Aware but feeling spacey. It's normal to feel out of place and not sure where or what to do. The experience of the higher dimensions is just that, there is no linear way of thinking. It just washes and can feel blank. It is like a sail boat out to sea and there are no winds. The boat moves back and forth, restless, the compass is spinning and yet you thought you had a specific place to go. All you can do is just stay calm, breathe and be in the moment. Experience the shifting and try not to react. Stay close to your community of like-minded who support each other. Keep things as simple as possible in your life because it will just wash away, out to sea. Just do the best you can with much self-love and trust that it is okay. Shine your light regardless no matter where or what you thought you were going to do. There is no schedule or an agenda to get stuff done. Just anchor and shine your beautiful light. As the commander of your ship, trust the seas and move with it, not against it.

Transformation

As your diet changes, you will be tuning more and more into what your body is telling you what it needs. Certain food, exercise, self-love. This is all healing as you begin to calibrate to the higher energies.

New Thoughts

Any thought that creates low vibrations is the most de-
structive energy one can impose on self and others. As our
emergence of becoming in to being as galactic humans,
we will illuminate only in accord with love and compassion.

Light or Dark?

When you find yourself engaging in thoughts that are not loving. As a creator you have a conscious choice to decide to change that vibration to love. Let go of whatever you hang on to. Just let go. Why create a reality that keeps you separated from yourself?

Kindness

One simple act of kindness, one word or phrase of being kind and loving each day impacts the world more than you know it. Try it.

It feels good just to be in your heart no matter where you are or what you are doing.

Change on this planet starts with each and every one of us doing just that.

Love is simple, powerful and healing.

Setting Yourself Free

If you are looking for a change in your life and feel stuck, then take one thing in your life that is a repeated pattern and has not allowed the change you desired.

Beliefs are Creations

Beliefs are everything from culture, religion, politics, daily living habits. Beliefs can distract you or enhance you. Do they cause you anger, pain, hurt verses love, joy and freedom?

As you evolve your daily habits of thoughts and behaviors will become transparent to you. You will see what you are creating and decide at that time if it is in your highest good.

Still Hanging On

If you are questioning a behavior of yours, then you are not ready to let go.

Integration

When functioning in your day to day activities, try to allow the heart to integrate and see how it affects everything you do.

Radio Dialing

Practice mindfulness by intentionally changing that pattern of thoughts and behaviors and do something different. It creates a different energetic frequency and thus changes your reality. It works.

Changing Your Frequency

You are a creator. Realities can be changed by thinking something differently and with intention. Why not try something just a little different today and every day and see what happens.

Strength

Empower yourself. It is not another entity that controls you anymore. Just the repeated pattern of thoughts. Get in the driver's seat of your life and set the course you choose to go to. Set yourself free and live like you have always wanted. When you realize how complicated we made our own life and become honest with what would really make you happy, it is not about materialistic things. It is about the experience of love in everything you do.

Oneness

It is not the competitions against each other, it is not the religious sectors believing one is right or better than another. It is just about love and one race. As humans on this planet, we want to be free and do what makes our hearts full.

Free Will Is A Choice

What is the driving force that keeps you creating day in and day out as we move into the New Earth? Is it the old paradigm of fear-based thinking? Or is it the new thoughts always being in a heart centered space?

Soar To New Heights

Envision how kindness rules and dismisses fear.
Fear that once ruled our lives and now obsolete.
Set yourself free and join humanity collectively to
being free, joyful and happy.

The Real You

Look beyond the routine of everyday life and see
the wonders of the world through your heart.

It is beautiful.

You are beautiful.

I AM

Love is a word that transmits the highest frequency of life. Love heals, love expands consciousness, Love is creation.

Love is the I AM presence of your God-self.

You are love.

Spend the day doing something loving for yourself. Feel the light of love pouring into you and through you. Have a date with nature and enjoy the elementals who are waiting for you to bring your light of love.

Division

Multi-tasking is a leaned behavior stem from fear-based thinking. It was designed to keep us separated from ourselves. We compartmentalized all the areas in our life to measure and generate the most productivity you can perform in one area. It became the norm and a noble thing in our society to sacrifice oneself to get so much done. The programming gives the illusion that you are a good person and that there are rewards. It really creates stress, sickness and disease due to the imbalances in our own energetic grid.

Slow down. Breathe and know that we are missing the true reason to be here on this beautiful planet.

Sending you waves of amazing light for clarity, calming seas to breathe and deep-rooted trees to anchor.

Bright Eyes

Can you imagine when the world collectively wakes up and decides to be free that our lives will never be the same again? What an exciting time to be here and to be part of such a huge historical event in our multiverse. Every one of us will/is a part of this process. No special class, initiation, group membership. Just be in your heart.

That is all and it is very powerful!!

Daily Thought

I live my life by choosing to be in the light all the time. Not when it is self-serving.

Separation of Self

Compartmentalization keeps you fragmented, distorted and separated. Find your thread of love and weave it all together.

That is all and it is very powerful!!

Integrating Light

Once above and below is now all integrated. Feel the light in your physical body. Feel the love that envelopes you with every cell. Floating, stillness, love and being free.

Own Your Light

Your existence is felt in the multi-verse. Your creations of every moment of every day impact all life all the time. Embrace who you are and how significant your presence brings to this time of great change.

Just For Today...

I am divinely ready to embrace all of me, wisdom, powerful force of light and love within me to serve my true purpose. I now embrace my collective selves and merge bringing forth the truth and wisdom in preparation for today.

I AM free to soar to the highest dimensional frequency.

I AM grateful, I AM joyful and I AM free.

Breaking Free

Timelines are controlled realms of limitations.

Journey

Take flight and experience the infinite of all knowing, all loving light of source.

"My heart is not just a vessel, but the bridge to love of the infinite world."

The Beginning

Compassion is the epicenter of releasing all
heaviness of our mis-creations.
Start with your inner self first.

Going Within

You now have permission to be the authority of your own life.

Do only what feels good, what's right.

If you are confused, fearful, then you are looking at the outside for answers and not going within.

You have to do the work to be free, happy and healthy.

We are waiting for you!

You

There is only one love. It is boundless, limitless
and complete.
Allow yourself to be Love

Healing More

Forgiveness has to start within. The old stories of pain are forced to the surface to heal, and release. No more hiding, but this time, just honor the lesson, the mis-creating and let it go. Allow it to gracefully be transmutated and bring more light in.

Your Choice

The rays of the Father Sun illuminate the path
for which you are seeking. However; it is you
who has to walk your path.

Getting Grounded

The trees are talking. They tower over you to protect, to nurture, to love. They are unconditionally loving and continue to wait for us to acknowledge them and their beauty. For today, acknowledge these amazing forms of life. They will hear you, they will feel you. They will appreciate your high vibrations.

New Day

Each new day is yesterday and tomorrow.
It continues each cycle with a new slate for new
creations with intentions.
Create wisely, lovingly and with your heart.

Star Gazing

A galactic human understands with compassion, wisdom and love. Forgiveness comes within and sees all life connected in the most beautiful ways. Feel the surge of life force energy pulsing through you and continues to the network of all life in the multiverse and being all life as one.

Wonderous, mystical, and so beautiful.

Let's Dance

Dance today like you have never danced before. Open your wings and feel the wind blow through you as you set flight. Laugh like you have never laughed before and feel the precious moment of just being in the now. Love with no exceptions, no limits, sending forth to all life with luminous light force energy.

Responsibility

Take a breath. Reset your mind. Control your vibrations with awareness and intentions. Create with the intention of creating for all.

Setting Intentions

What are you thinking?

Is it with mindfulness? The waves of light coming from your thoughts are creating instantly.

> Is it with love?
> Is it from your heart?
> Is it for the greatness of the higher vibrations of all life?

Create with passion, love and heart.

Remember who you are and why you are here in the bigger picture.

Stay connected to your divine self all the time.

Change will only happen if each of us do our work.

Change within us and this planet is imminent.

Love, Service and Wisdom

Being of Service

Step from your self-focus and practice being of service.

The view of your own paradigm will change with such gratitude, love and joy helping others!

Today, I will practice doing acts of kindness.

Compassion

Becoming a master is one who listens more than one speaks. One creates room in the inner self that is filled with light. One reflects other's words and has patience. Processing of self is not the majority of one's time rather practicing stillness and being in the moment of just being.

Tranquil

The quality of a human being craves peace. Create the world that allows your God-self to create that peace within you and on the planet.

Be Love

To be free is to not volunteer enslavement.

It is a choice. Together we can make an impact.

Unity, consciousness and love.

Dig Deeper

Today and just for today —

Practice looking at things from a much different perspective.

Pay attention to those things that draw you in and keep you separated from a place of love, your higher self.

Feel the incredible strength of your I AM presence taking over and flood you with oneness.

Connected to all that there is.

When you become more aware of the things around you that don't feel loving, then simply practice perspective. Removing your energetic self, your emotional side and not engage.

See things with compassion and that we all are trying to emerge into oneness. Together, collectively. We all are sharing this most amazing time of change. It is a time of allowing.

Embrace your Galactic Self as a creator. Being Galactic simply means moving from the dense paradigm of duality, a 3-dimensional platform, to a place of love and being in a higher dimension from the process of evolution.

213

Perception

How you live your life is mirrored from
Mother Earth.

Bliss

Today, just for today, despite all the noise and distractions around you, cut yourself loose and envision life on Earth as pure love, freedom, abundance, laughter. No rules, no competition, no violence.

Just be in the bliss of the I AM state.

Present

Act vs react. Intent vs lack of ownership. Be vs waiting. Just live now.

The Truth Is Revealed

Everything that existed in your eyes will fall away, like an illusion that magically fades, revealing the most incredible light one has ever seen.

Taking Flight

The only one controlling your own
evolution is you. Embrace your creative
abilities and take off the chains yourself.
You are holding yourself back. Let go
of it all and just feel yourself merging
with your higher self.

Think Great Thoughts

Every little positive change you make in your life increases your own frequency and Mother Earths. Vibrate high!

Paying Attention

The 3D world, as we know it, is merely reflecting back the very vibration we emit, thus creating the reality we experience. Nothing just happens to us, rather we create that happening. Look at the inanimate objects around you in your life, flat tire, water leak in the house, things break. Even your physical body will communicate with your imbalances. They are frequencies we emit out like an antenna. It is energy speaking to you.

Removing Blocks

Energies that move from different timelines are coming to form now. The Cause and Effect. Everything is not always instantaneous. We cause our own delay to desire new creations by the self-imposed limiting beliefs. Learning to let go is one of humanities biggest challenges.

Balancing

What an opportunity to acknowledge the imbalances and heal.

Everything is mirroring the very energy we emit that allows us to see what is not in harmony or in balance with our life.

This is the greatest chance to acknowledge the imbalances and heal.

Family

Peace is a natural state of a galactic human.
One who ripples waves of light that draws others of the
same vibration.

Dive Into The Ocean Of Light

Taking a deep breath of awareness is
calming, quiet and peaceful.

Integrating Light

As your soul-self sloths off the old energies during the emergence. You will seek quiet places. A tree, a hike, a swim. Feel the urge, acknowledge it and do the right thing for your soul self that is incorporating a whole new awareness.

Sage

Speak minimally. Listen attentively.
Love freely. Create intentionally.
You are Source.

Truth

Practice peace until you can trust this is
your true state of being.

Balancing

We cannot be happy in one place in
our life by compartmentalization.
The challenge is to be happy in
everything we do.

Casting Light
Onto The Shadows

The darkest places in our life are the areas
we perhaps need to focus on to heal.
Not to separate further from oneself.

Fragmented To Freedom

If one stays separated from oneself,
living a life of compartmentalization, we
will always have a difficult time tapping
into our own divine wisdom.

Community Of Light

Separation from our higher self, prevents the divine collective from coming in.

We will have a difficult time being a total light to the collective. We cannot merge in totality of the collective until we can merge all of ourselves. Pulling back and centering the fragments and distortions of frequencies from our thoughts, words and actions and then maintaining this vibration to embrace the I AM presence.

Keep practicing a place of stillness, no matter how noisy it may be. Be patient. It is work. We all have to do it to make the change for a new reality.

One of infinite light, love, Divine Grace in all that we do.

We need each other to make this great change. We are brothers and sisters sharing, supporting and allowing each of us to walk and work our own divine paths no matter how far or close we are in our progress of illumination.

Be patient, gentle and loving yourself and everyone you meet today.

The Shaman

Sometimes there are no explanations. It just is.

Accepting and allowing. Embracing and loving. These present times have been the most challenging with our own letting go. A roller coaster ride with Mother Earth. The life times of holding and carrying the old energies forward is and has been forced to the surface. It has wreaked havoc and at times we wonder how much more pain can we take. What always keeps us going is our will and passion for life and the gift and opportunity to be here and do what we came here to do.

Our journey continues to teach us the infinite realms that have been hidden from all of us.

No human can conceptualize the depth of old energies that lie dormant in our cells and think that we can be freed without feeling anything. This teaches us a deeper level of compassion to ourselves and life. We are eternally grateful to God that we feel closer and closer to our emergence of the I AM.

The physical and emotional pain that surfaces are the old energies. Go into the pain and send your light there. Forgiveness and love. Compassionate and caring for your vessel like you have never have before. It is merely the intention and focus on that old energy to be released.

Set everything free that you have held on to for it serves no purpose. There is no more reason to have fear and to cling. Trust who you are and believe you are the light, source and creator.

Look Within
To See Your Truth

Measuring or comparing yourself to someone or something else is dishonoring who you already are.

Measuring and comparing someone or something else to who you are is dishonoring them and yourself.

A state of allowing is honoring all that there is.

Separation from others is a separation of self.

We are all One.

Going Home

Stepping forward into the light
I melt away the layers of lifetimes
of limited beliefs, worries, doubts and
fears. I see the fragments of thoughts
that I have carried and have plagued me
with repetition. Like an old movie of pain. I
carried them for such a long time.

I let go with tears.

I surrendered it all for a chance to finally see who I AM.

The I AM that has been stuffed away for so long. Pushed
in the back in layers of life times and continued habits of
not letting go. Surrounded by material things, distractions
and with energy of thought forms that manifested the
continued state of existence.

Now not holding on to anything but my heart. I have
surrendered everything on a cellular level to take flight and
be light once again.

I walk and breathe completely and fully. A higher frequency
and different dimension I can call home. I AM.

Engagement of Love

When I close my eyes, I see the grid line around the Earth. I see it glowing golden crystalline energy. I see pillars of lights rise above and connect into the grid. I feel the surge of love that cannot be explained. Not a rush, not overwhelming, just sweet calmness and joy.

Smiling, laughing. Feelings like a newborn that has not yet been tainted with the old programming and manipulation of genetic and psychological alterations. A new born that carries the pure light, pure essence of God is in each and every one of us. Our light that was once in the darkness of our self-made shadows is now illuminated. It relinquishes control of heavy energies and disintegrates the paradigm of enslavement.

The strong solar and heart rays ascend upon us.

There is no turning back now. Knowing of the now is all that one can possibly need or desire.

Stand tall and look around. See with the eyes that gave us the ability create a realm that combines everything your heart ever desired. Everything. For we are the extension in physical form of creator.

... Engagement of Love

You are a being so incredibly powerful. Powerful to create the storms, the winds, the rains. Powerful to melt the fear away. Powerful to touch all life here on Gaia and see herself in all of her glory. Communing with the elements and life as it is a part of us.

Close your eyes to see the reality that does exist in your heart. Walk away from every tie to pain and control as it is time for no more suffering.

Be in joy, love, freedom and happiness.

Kindness is the breeze that gently sweeps your soul and clears the debris.

Be Gentle With Yourself

Today, I wish you joy, calmness and peace within. Some days it will appear as the same "stuff" that you cannot control. But how you handle it differently will reflect from your own growth. What a wonderful thing to see!

Raise The Flag To Reclaim Yourself!

Know that the struggle we are having is not simply diagnosed by the seasons or holidays, or a condition rather it is healing. The resistance and the fight to let go feels like we are transitioning. Being exhausted from the continuous cycles of low energy daily patterns was accepted as the norm for humanity. But the resistance never resonated with our natural state of being.

Stay strong, dig deep. Remember who we are and how powerful we are. Especially during this time. The high frequencies are intense, and it is literally pulling all the old energies off of us.

Let it go.
Just breathe and let it go.
Breathe. Let it go.
Feel the calmness come over and allow our higher self to jump in the driver seat. Ego step aside.

Drive! Drive into the winds of life and feel the breeze cleansing our soul. Feel the warmth of the sun penetrating and activating our DNA on a cellular level. Nothing more beautiful then the grace upon us and being one with all. We all are here together. No one is alone. Breathe and feel us.

You are so very much loved!

If you seriously want change, look at what we are creating in our own life today. Why are we not feeling well, or truly happy. Change can only happen if you create it.

Unified As Light

Simple changes can be to embrace all of your collective selves into your I AM presence and reclaim your right here as a Galactic Human.

Be The Example

Practice freedom by smiling at strangers, eliminating contracts that bind us, mindful of the entertainment and how it really affects your vibration. Be outside and connect to Mother Earth as she is waiting for a loving vibrational hug from you.

We welcome you with open arms and an open heart. We wait for you to embrace your I AM presence and jump on board to the life we truly desire and deserve.

From Surviving To Thriving

The change reminds me of swimming in a vast ocean that the shores on each end (paradigms) are getting further and further away from each other.

Fear still lingers deeply and rooted in those attempting to not swim. Transparency reveals the weights one carries and slows them down. Fighting the change, trying to control and feeling tired.

Breathe through each stroke and allow the divine light to enter in.

Every stroke made is closer to your I AM presence. See your own shadows be released as if they were anchors that did not serve you any longer. Replace the anchors (weights of heaviness and old energies) with self-love and allow the lightness of Source take over.

You are almost there, do not give up.

Stay in stillness, keep swimming and breathing through every stroke, every effort.

You will not be left behind.

Source is right there with you.

Just Observing

That art of allowing is just being in a state of stillness. Not engaging in other's beliefs, their programming and their training. (So yes, use discernment with every person, everything you read, been taught and know).

Student of Life

The art of allowing is becoming the master of your own awakening. First and foremost, own who you are. A creator. Then allow your own layers to continue to be released, yes, it will shake your current state of comfort, and it will not feel easy because we are still accustomed to linear way of thinking and feeling. An illusion of safety.

Follow Your Light

Your innate self is propelling you forward and wanting unification of all of your collective selves to connect with Source.

The ability to create is the path of least resistance. Are you still struggling in places of your life?

Merging

Start by incorporating parts of you in your 3 dimensional realm and see yourself flourishing to infinite possibilities.

Breathe

If you are feeling stuck, just be still and look at everything. Release what no longer serves you and remember who you are.

You are Light

Love yourself as you are like no other.

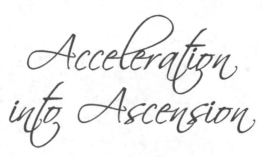

Acceleration into Ascension

Pain and Spirituality

Being in the state of emotional pain and observing oneself experience the pain is different.

How can you control to be in one state or the other?

You can't.

It is spiritual maturity that will give you the perspective from the higher dimension.

Humanity will continue to endure the pain experience.

It will however not keep your vibration down, but the shifted perspective and the spiritual maturity will allow all things to be viewed differently, thus a release will occur much quicker once the enlightenment of that experience can puncture the seal of confinement.

It will also propel one further into ascension due to the release of that pain and gainfully embracing that experience.

Infinite You Are!

There is so much more of you waiting to join
your merging of light.

Consciousness

Close your eyes and feel with your heart.
Feel the shifting taking place deep within
you. Feel all parts of you float away and more
love comes in. Connected and free.

Going Home

The only reason we are here is to ascend. Be one with source and all life.

The power of the mind is controlled by your beliefs.

You decide what you choose to engage in (Free will).

You will be tested and distracted continually by things that make you sad, fearful and angry.

Observe, send light, pray and meditate where it is needed, refrain from engaging.

Be mindful of your super human abilities and where you draw your attention to.

News, technologies, sickness and disease.
This is a manipulation tactic that will attempt to control your creative energies.

Bullet Train

You are controlling your own evolution. By choosing what you eat, what you think, what you create determines the acceleration process.

Taking Flight

Ascension is not something given to us, rather it is our own awakening process of becoming into full consciousness. It takes will, determination and trust to merge into the light that we call home.

Ownership

Be your own truth
Not someone else's

Walking the Rainbow Bridge

Huge, huge shifting taking place right now. Get grounded. Stay centered. 3D is fracturing and so many are not awake to understand what is happening. Be mindful to stay detached and have compassion. Keep your vibration higher than you ever have. Laugh, smile, choose to be happy. The wave is so much easier to ride!

Create Responsibly

What you think is what you create.

What is going on within you will reflect your creation.

Choosing sides to anything will only enforce the division from your higher self and with humanity. Dividing yourself limits your full potential to be that amazing light.

Focus on how you want to choose to live now.

Freedom, Health and LOVE.

Removing Your 3D Veil

Unfoldment of the universal truth will be revealed to us all. First you have to surrender all beliefs before you can see what is right in front of you.

Quiet Please

Practicing stillness is the only way to hear
your higher self speak wisdom.

Flower Blooming

Merging of our collective selves brings us
completeness and graduating to our
I AM presence.

Feeling Heavy

The only blockage to full consciousness is
any limiting belief that gets in the way.

Setting Sail

Everything is perfect and will be okay.
Breathe.

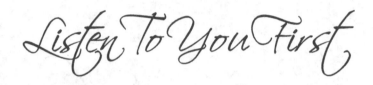

Listen To You First

Be the most beautiful powerful light that you are.

Trust your own abilities of insight, intuition and love to find truth in everything.

This is the only way to make change here on Earth.

Practice stillness, self-love and compassion to all.

Loving Light

God, Source, Creator Cares.
That is what matters.

Unified Abundance

Allow your heart to fill with infinite love.
Then you can experience life as you dreamt about.

Removing the Blockage

Your own merge with your collective selves can happen now if you change your daily routine. Daily routines create duality and block your higher self from penetrating your heart.

Letting Go

Any sort of judgement during the ascension process will severely harm you. Be careful of what you think. Be transparent. Be love.

Rays of Light

There is only one of you here.
Make it count.

Life

Dreams are to be experienced
Realities are to be created
Create your dream reality

Powerful

Isolate not to avoid.
Disengage the matrix that was designed to keep you
separated from your higher self,
We can still feel and hear you
You are not alone
Unplug from the wall
Plug in to yourself and listen.

Listen

It is quieter now
Can you feel everything?
Can you see everything?
Do you know everything?

Discernment

Surrender is not to give up.
But to stop resisting the change we always wanted.
We are creating the change.

Wisdom

Choose to engage your energy wisely.

Ask yourself, does it serve a higher purpose?

Will it affect my own vibration?

What would it serve?

Try to be in stillness and just observe, without judgement.

Learn patience of yourself and others.

Spend time learning to love yourself rather than being distracted by the outside.

It is about developing a relationship with yourself, like never before.

Your higher-self stepping in and taking control to see things with a shifted perspective.

It is all about love, the infinite realms and being joyful without expectation of a person, place or thing.

Enlightment

May the light fall on your shoulders every moment of everyday showing clarity, happiness, joy and love!

Take The Leap

We are here and awake now.
Rise, Rise, Rise.
It is time for change.

You Are Magical!

Practice unplugging from the electronic world and plug in to your higher self. All you need to know is within you.

Love yourself, trust yourself and embrace who you are.

Your authentic self. All loving, all knowing, Divine Light!

Becoming a Master

Shadows surface and disappear as quickly as they come and go.

Body opens to more light as the release continues.

Stepping into confidence and trust that the bridge will hold you as you continue to walk your path.

Breathe and feel it. All the way down. Breathe more. Be still.

Smile. Be compassionate. Smile at the simplest things.
Be aware of all the paradigms around you, but only chose the one you want to engage in.

A creator. A galactic human. An embodiment of the light. Feel the shimmering effect of the change within you chemically. Your body is now morphing to crystalline energy.

Diets are changing, and your body will tell you what it can and cannot process.

Organs will disintegrate based on the higher level of light you become.

Density cannot be process. Watch the programming fight to control your will, your desire. Your freedom.

Be, feel and live your passion. Become who want to become.

Freedom to just be. Laugh.

Feel. Time disappears, and it only exists to measure productivity in the 3D world.

Love with all of you and walk in gratitude to be a part of something so much more than we could have ever imagine.

Surrendering

If you are still experiencing body or emotional pain and are trying to release it through prayer and meditation, then there are areas still in your life that you may have not surrendered.

Awareness

You know by now what beliefs and actions are limiting by being in the 3D. It's difficult as that is how most of us were taught to live by. Our Higher Self is now taking over and the tug of war is happening with the Ego.

Being in the Light

Trust, believe and know that however we have lived before is not working, has never worked and it is time to step in the driver's seat and go within to the all knowing, all loving connection of your I AM self.

Clearing

In order for your vessel to be free of any limitations, these frequencies (pains) still being manifested can be released by going deep in your heart and totally surrender. The pains are merely reminding us that our work is not done in this part of our ascension.

Ripple Effect

Take a look at your life. Be that creator and consciously examine all vibrations you are creating.

Desire

Practice daily to be aware of your behaviors and implement change immediately. This will allow new frequencies that can be reprogrammed to change your manifestations in a more favorable creation of your life.

One of your choosing.

Mirroring Light

Practice peace within and see your reality change to reflect your most inner self. Love

Intense Change

As your body continues to morph from carbon to crystalline, different things will be experienced. Body pain, illness, tiredness. The body has to go through quite a bit of changes to become more light. It holds life times of memories and programming. So all of this has to be released if it is not serving your ascension.

All current discords in your life has to come to a resolve in order for you to continue on your light path. These imbalances will get obvious and loud in your life that you cannot but help to take action to heal and release these parts. It will become very uncomfortable trying to hang on to them. Honor it and let it go. Your body is trying to catch up with your higher self.

Getting into Alignment

All energetic layers will start to sync up with your highest vibration. Any programming that surfaces that brings discord or affects your vibration will be apparent and stand out more now than ever. Just acknowledge it and be in gratitude for the experience and let it go.

Cleansing

Call on Archangel Michael and his sword of light to clear and remove any remaining heavy energies that have been in-bedded for life times. I use the Violet Flame/Fire daily to help transmute these energies. Being lighter now, over 51%, will allow you to experience increased moments of bliss, love and joy.

New Gifts Arriving!

Your own vibration will start to affect the physical paradigm around you, i.e. items moving without touching them (telekinesis), experiencing more activity in other dimensions.

Practice Just Being

Just observing with non-judgement and not being a part of it. Walking with your light and allow it to expand outward to Mother Earth and all life is the most powerful action you can do right now. Anchor it deeply. Have trust, believe more now than ever that everything is happening perfectly in divine order.

Setting The Example

Practice mindfulness by responding with 5 dimensional thoughts and behaviors in your life. It is like learning to ride a bicycle in a totally different way. Easier and more fun! Imagine that!

It changes everything.

Awareness

The biggest and most precious gift you can do for yourself and Mother Earth is radiate LOVE. That is all you need to do to be free of this heavy paradigm of enslavement.

Love makes your heart pound with infinite light.

Fear confines your light and creates distortions, doubt and staying out of balance with life.

Moving through the Cosmic Waves of Ascension

As each person progresses to the higher frequencies, it is imperative to stay grounded.

There is much going on of every level of your being and with Mother Earth.

It takes constant conscious effort to keep cleaning your energetic fields daily.

As the light intensifies, it will continue to penetrate deeper and deeper within our energetic bodies, thus revealing layer upon layer old energies that surface. Some injuries and pains will go away, new ones will appear.

Especially for empaths, the days are going to be more dramatic in our emotional states. Feelings of depression, questioning your existence, perhaps moments of feeling like losing your mind, and a big one for most, feeling lonely.

You may have a partner, spouse or even a family, you may be living alone, regardless, the feeling can be intense at times when you feel no one "gets" you. But remember, most will feel something like this on some level, but perhaps will not be able to identify it.

This is the "void" state where one is being stripped of the paradigm of the old energies, i.e. thought forms, habits, patterns of behavior. Moments of forgetfulness. Strange things that are daily routine will be thrown off, even missing memory.

Work with your guides more now than ever as they will assist you while we all are walking in this tunnel of transition on a conscious level. It is an unknown path for us as our 3D abilities will not work here during this time anymore. We know intuitively the light is there and very near for our complete shift into the higher dimension.

Foods are going to be more and more difficult to find what your body needs versus what we read or what we are told. Remember, live, green foods are higher energy and is what all bodies need. But your mind (ego) may fight you due to the addictions. Your body eventually will not be able to assimilate these foods and will revolt. (As mine did the other day).

Be outside every chance you get. Look at your priorities and ask if it is serving your higher purpose at this moment. What is the most important thing for you at this moment? I felt so strongly to be outside with Mother Earth, to breathe and just be. I know from here on out that every effort I work on my ascension, it is accelerating a thousand-fold times faster.

Ask your guides for the downloads that are needed at this time. Ask that all this shifting is done with ease and grace so that the impact is not harsh. Remember, as bad as some of us want to just move into this higher frequency, all of us (Body, mind and spirit) are inclusive and have to shift to this same frequency. Hence the body being the densest, the mind releasing layers of programming of lifetimes. It is not an overnight process or a weekend event. It is mostly up to you and the work you put forth. Your will.

Call on the Creator, your guides (Company of Heaven), your Star Brothers and Sisters of the Light. They can only assist if you ask them.

With Much Love and Light and Gratitude,

Cheryl

ABOUT CHERYL GALL

Cheryl's background is quite unique. She is a master healing practitioner, teacher and consultant. She is clairsentient, claircognizant, empathic and intuitive and has been practicing energy healing for over 25 years. Cheryl's work focuses on the assistance of healing humanity and Mother Earth for ascension. Cheryl has a unique energy signature that makes it possible for others to experience major shifts in their lives resulting from her light work.

Cheryl practices and is certified in Peruvian Shamanic Practices and Reiki Master. She holds a B.S. in Occupational Studies. Cheryl has a vast and successful careers being in the US Marines, Aerospace Industry, Corporate, Retail, Law Enforcement, Insurance Investigations, and having her own personal training business that allows her to have the ability to reach a wide variety of clients in different places in their lives.

Cheryl has been a guest speaker on internet radio shows, to name a few, "Metaphysical Talk Radio" and "Just the Debs" as well as speaking engagements with local businesses in Southern California. She has been published in the Sedona Journal Magazine and continues to write inspirations that will assist with others shifting of consciousness.

Cheryl strives to practice living a true balance in her life by incorporating body, mind, and spirit discovering a complete sense of self-empowerment as she embodies ascension in her own path. She is passionate about sharing her skills and personal experience with others who are searching to improve their own life and become a healthier, happier being.

9 780578 741994